Traveling On

POEMS BY DUANE R. CHRISTIANSON

TRAVELING ON
LYRIC POETRY

iUniverse books may be ordered through booksellers or by contacting:

iUniverse
1663 Liberty Drive
Bloomington, IN 47403
www.iuniverse.com
844-349-9409

ISBN: 978-1-6632-2200-8 (sc)
ISBN: 978-1-6632-2201-5 (e)

Print information available on the last page.

iUniverse rev. date: 06/18/2021

About the Author

⁓

DUANE R. CHRISTIANSON lives in Davidson, NC with his wife Toni Youngblood. He moved here from Oak Park, Illinois.

This is his second book of poetry, the first being "Burning on the Mesa." He retired from the Veterans Administration in 2010 and has had time as well as encouragement to write more poetry since then.

He describes his career as a series of caroms between occupations. His poems also disclose tangentially his experience in studying English, his work as a piano tuner-technician, as a job placement counselor, and subsequently as a job modifier using adaptive computer technology for the blind. He spent thirty years working in the field of blind rehabilitation.

Today, he tells his grandchildren. "Find something that has no solution but that needs one badly. Throw your heart into it."

In many ways this also explains his love of poetry: "I have always liked playing with words, their sounds, images, and music, and especially when suddenly, by choice or chance, they are put together in such a way that they illuminate my life, and the lives of others. May these poems reach my readers in the way that they reach me."

Acknowledgments

~

"Traveling On" would not appear without the encouragement of Professor Colin Campbell and Professor Anthony Abbott over the years in writing poetry. I also owe a substantial debt to Clark Beim-Esche who had faith in me and in these poems, paid scrupulous attention to the text, and made invaluable suggestions.

I have been a member of a local poetry-writing group for several years in Davidson. Its members have been a source of good company, good poetry, and good criticism for which I am thankful. Lastly, I must thank my wife, Toni Youngblood, for reviewing poems, energetically encouraging me to write, and to produce a book. If there is a muse discernable behind the poems in this book, one kinder and gentler than in "Burning on the Mesa," it is my wife.

"Crazy Old Men," and "Descending with the Goth" appeared in "Burning on the Mesa." "You Can Do Anything You Want Now" has been changed to "Grandfather Eric." I trust all three poems are improved.

Contents

~

For Toni

Traveling On

This train might, just might,
wait a while for you,
but you two can't wait for it.

Are you surprised you've lost
the baggage of old griefs?
Did you imagine once
that they'd sustain you?
You will find now
what you need
in where and how
you choose to go.

On this late afternoon,
steel rails blaze golden in the light,
but seem to come together
long before they reach
a wedge of cloud
that hovers in the West.
You know that threatened end
of journeying in its
too easy mockery of sight.

A wide country will roll past you
mile on unfamiliar mile.
Out on the plains at night,
expect to feel
your new wife's arms around you,

the rocking motion of the train.
You'll see small running lights display
what comes closest as you pass.
Look out into darkness of the plains.
It's there that farm lights,
however widely set apart
will look like bright umbrellas
set up against the dark.

Somehow you may think
that they hold up the sky.

3/25/2021

I

Sun Dial in Cornelius, North Carolina

Memoir Assignment

We'll talk about our lives eventually—
but don't expect
we'll wave our hands
as if we were in class.

We'll frame what we should say
a thousand times,
then stumble back a thousand more
through what's not yet completely worn away:
old landmarks in the heart,
the paths we took,
and rough-edged maps
for which you haven't asked
of where the sweet streams ran
and where perhaps as well
the dragons lay.

9/11/2020

Crazy Old Men

Crazy old men
rise late, rise early
or keep reading through the night,
may not wonder why
the sign-off pattern
on the TV has
long since disappeared,
can't figure out,
when the coffee's brewed,
why no one they have loved
descends the stairs.

Crazy old men
forget to act their age,
want muscle cars,
young women,
not now,
not now,
but then,
back then
in their teens and twenties,
the time that they despair
somehow had escaped them,
want to remember
what it was to be chasing
and then being chased,
being at least
one time
prized.

Crazy old men sometimes
wake out of fantasies
of meeting their first loves,
stumble forward
as if on slippered feet
toward the recollections
that, unlike women,
don't have
bags to pack
or anywhere to go.

Crazy old men want
to get up and dance,
ricochet off walls in polkas,
swing on vines
through jungle canopies,
feel guts jump up
as they pitch forward
through the air.

Crazy old men tire out
just like the rest of us,
but sooner.
They settle down,
invest in beachfront properties,
knowing sea-rise
will not come for them,
plant lounges and umbrellas
on ocean-facing yards
as if creating gardens

that will always be attended to,
place tables where
they can see how
light reflects the colors
of a rosé in a glass.

And they'll hope for sun
to dispense its mercy,
rest gently, gently
on broad white hats
and browning arms.

One by one
crazy old men
may reach out for sanity,
but only in the a quiet
they have chosen
for themselves,
perhaps want pens,
then, paper,
maybe a computer.

They'll wonder if they
can figure out
old reel-to-reel recorders,
if the ten-year-olds can really teach them
what to do with video.
Recollections of old times
call them back
to other places,

passions, angers, dreams.
They curse and bless
and sometimes hide from memory.

But then they write,
just may, then speak or try
and fail to tell it all.

It's just another sign of madness,
but it is their own,
somehow declaring,
"In the writing,
in the saying,
I was,
I am,
I will be,
by God,

Alive!"

3/18/2021

An Afternoon Rain

He cannot see the rain.
It is that thin and clear
as it moves without drama
toward a line of sun-lit trees.
It seems to wipe his hands
of heat and this day's cares.
Something in the woodland
offers light applause.

7/1/2020

II

Stockholm Harbor

The Tourist

I did not come
for mountain air or thawing out.
I am not scaling boulders barefoot
in some mad ascent.

I have no plans for blasting prairie dogs
from Colorado into outer space
because it's what the locals do.
And I'm not jumping off a plane
so, I can get in touch
with that far place
from which I came
at three times highway speed.

Feel free to dive headfirst from bridges
while attached to Bungee cords.
You can tell me later
that you found something primal
when you almost kissed a rock.

But don't you ever think
that I am doing nothing here.
On late nights up Spring Creek Mesa
or maybe up on Sunset
when city lights have failed
to bleach the sky

sometimes I'll look and find Orion,
or perhaps the Bear, and spot

another tourist
hanging out awhile among,
but different from, the stars.

4/9/2021

A Postcard from the West

A brush fire set the railroad bridge
alight on River Walk.
And there are piles of wood chips
still smoldering north of town.

The winds have kept us both
indoors for days,
but no fires have come near.

One preacher on the TV
says, "Expect the Rapture
in a couple days."
Still, I think the world
is too uneventful
to end as fast as that.

The stove pipe can't give up
its steady moan.
We thumb through aging catalogs,
tie fishing flies,
watch a rabbit in the yard—
ears up for danger,
its tail to the wind.

3/4/2021

Old Irish Cemetery

It must be hard to run a mower here,
just getting to the few grass plots
among the Celtic crosses
jammed together upright,
none prostrate on the ground.
They form a bristling company
of those who wait the final trumpet call.

Back in the States,
our plots accommodate caretakers.
Grave stones lie flat along the ground.
How can we know what those
who lie beneath them may expect?
the trumpet's call on some transcendent morning
or just the passing roar of mower blades?

3/5/2020

In Galway

Sometimes it's only afterwards,
you notice
as on the day you made it quick-time
with a tour guide heading
straight for Galway Bay
where she said there were
historic things we ought to see.

But you remember nothing
of what she showed you,
only what you glimpsed in passing:
how a bearded man
with no printed sign that might
plead for help
slumped back against the wall
before a store
that was called The Wooden Heart.

He knew what he was doing,
knew someone at least
might leave some coins
so he could feed the dog
that slept beside him on the walk.

You didn't have a Euro,
had nothing you could give,
and knew you would lose your guide

if you paused for a second,
thinking you might talk.

But you were with a gang of Yanks,
hurried, always hurried in and through
somebody's disappearing history,
charging past the Wooden Heart—
doors not yet opened on a Sunday—
to reach a waiting bus.

2/5/2021

The Taj Mahal 1

On the Bus in Delhi

Once on the hired bus,
we watch Shiva's six-inch statue
on the dashboard
point our way through streets
we've never seen before.
Our guide names the places
we will not recall.

He won't think to tell us,
and we won't think to ask
why the women
just ahead of us in saris,
bright green and red,
ride through the city
in a dump truck
uncovered in the rain.

3/19/2021

Tyger, Tyger

The man in saffron robes declares
it is only out of fear
we refuse to be the tiger's lunch.

He's partly right,
and perhaps someday
I might have to make
my objections clear
in double-barreled lead
if I walked
the Ranthambore Preserve alone.

Just now, I remember
an old tigress in the woods.
She wanted deer:
sambar, spotted, barking.
It didn't matter.
A sacrificial goat would do.
So too would carrion.

I don't believe
she had too much more
on her mind that morning,
not even, "Damn the monkeys
for scaring off the deer!"
much less how she
could unify me with the universe.

Hunger said, it wanted deer,
a sacrificial goat or carrion.

The man in saffron robes declares again
it is only out of fear
we refuse to be the tiger's lunch.

If the great Oneness is carnivorous,
I will have none of it.
And as long as I
can load and fire off objections,
it won't have much of me.

8/3/2020

Boat on the Mekong in Cambodia

Cambodia

You cannot pass this by
as you leave a village
whose name in Khmer
you can't remember now:
the dozen blankets
spread out by smiling children
on the Mekong's bank,
the bright colors of silk scarves
declaring life against
a background of crushed grass.

You know you have
been called here

by something other than
the captain or your tour guide.

Small hands reach out,
brown, sticky, in a sun
you haven't seen before—
for its brightness—
for its heat—
and for its lack of mercy.

Buy something quick
before too many kids
wave silken wares before your eyes—
in green, blue, yellow, red—
their patterns dazzling in the light—
before the children all rush in—
select you among the wandering Yanks
to make a sale,
take prices down,
call out, "Six dollar, four,—
three, two,—
Please, mister,"—
before your money disappears,
before you—
unsteady on the muddy, tilted stairs
leading to the Mekong—
get back into the safety
of your craft,
before you know
there is nothing left to offer

the children of this country—
for the moment—
but the poem you will write
in blessing them.

2/8/2021

III

In Quarantine

Nothing's moving in the woodland,
but heat pours up at you
from the parking lot.
Car windows stare into naked sky
with their bright and blinding eyes.

7/13/2020

A Letter to Whoever Is in Charge

Dear Sir or Madam:

Give me my old life back.
Yes, please, please.
All of it.
It was stopped by proclamation
back in March.

I want to hear
the crickets chirp more loudly.

I want tree frogs
to tune up in mass chorus,
tires to hiss at night on pavement
shining bright with rain.
I want to hear my neighbors' gossip
through the windows,
the metal whirr of roller skates,
the sound bikes make
when dropped down onto walks.

Give me the crack of bats in sandlots,
children shouting everywhere.
I even miss how loudly they
call each other names.

Where have the dragsters gone?
I'll settle for the sound of spinning tires,
cars passing with bad mufflers
that months ago
was sure to bring down the cops.

I'll gladly take jack hammers early mornings,
pile drivers slamming into rock,
whatever whistles, honks or makes
us know that there is life.

Give me parades
with Kodo drummers,
pounding out some rhythms
I haven't known before,
and high school bands
well out of tune,
but playing Souza.

I don't ask much.
Let me see a half-time show.
I don't care who's playing,
It doesn't matter
the yard line I am on.
Just let someone reach a row
that's somewhere near me,
calling in whatever outdoor voice

that's left to him
after the long silence
we have all endured,
"Pretzels,
Pretzels,
Beer!"

I'll know the world is back then,
and me too.

5/20/2021

The Escape

Don't say you can't imagine this:
the day's heat etched in black tar
that's melting on the street;
the August air filled up
with what it can't forget
of gentle late-night rains;
and yards away a woodland
that seems baked
into the stillness
of a painting on a wall.

Don't say you can't imagine this:
your need to challenge your restraints
and fears you cannot name.

You'll reach the wood
and touch its leaves,
the bark of oaks and pine.

Don't say you can't imagine this:
the sudden coolness of the trees,
light airs that offer light embrace,
the murmured invitation from a creek
to see and hear it flowing
toward a pool so deep and wide
that you could freely swim.

Don't say you can't imagine this:
a slide into the stream,
cold water rising past your knees,
the chance to play
in splashing, tossing pebbles
at anything you like
as when you were a child,
and whooping in pure glee.

Don't say you can't imagine this:
the angled climb you'll take at last
through mud and twigs and vines
that seek to keep you
in a dappled light
safe from the shock of sun.

Don't say you can't imagine this:
the sight of smiling men
in wilted uniforms
who are walking toward you now,
their arms outspread as if—
absurdly in the heat—
insisting on a hug.

3/19/2021

IV

The Ice Age

At ten, you could not know for sure
what might happen
if the ice came back,
but your science textbook offered clues.
As for detail, you knew
what you could guess:

Guess that your music teacher'd interrupt
the class as car horns began blaring
in massed chorus from the road.

Guess that you and everybody else
would rush the windows,
stare at the traffic heading south—
in a kind of multi-colored sludge—
with no one heading toward Wisconsin
and a brilliant line of white.

Guess how the radio'd come on
with someone sounding,
all grown up, relaxed,—
perhaps a baritone—
saying everything was fine—
yes, really, really fine.

Guess that he'd be lying
and that your parents

would be lying too—
whenever they'd arrive.
Guess that you'd see geese
high up at night against the Moon,
hear them calling to each other—
and to you—
as they started heading South.

Oh, you wished back then
to meet the eyes
of shambling, hairy beasts
from your upstairs window,
hoped you'd hear them
lumbering through the night.

You wished all that
but yet somehow you knew,
even at ten, you knew
no moon could gleam again
off twelve-foot tusks,
curved and long
as ancient instruments,
knew that there could be—
no waking ever—
to mammoths' trumpeting.

3/19/2021

A Petition

Mrs. Bass,
can we put off a week,
or, better still, a year,
that film that's called,
"Where Babies Come From"?
You put it on your schedule,
but it's not on ours.
Go play it one more time
for the kids in Seventh Grade
who keep staring at each other
as if they've found some mystery.

We have a schedule
you don't know about
or want to:
taking sleds on sheer ice
down Killer Hill out back,
shooting baskets in the gym
when we should be waiting for the bus,
and then there is trying
to pump hard enough
on rusty swings
so they'll go parallel,
or, better still, straight over.

And you don't know
how much we want

the key to that place
with the "No Admittance" sign
that leads to the subbasement.

We even know about the tunnel
leading down the front hill to the river.
We'll crawl on hands and knees
to reach the entrance on the bank
nobody's reached in years.
There must be clues all over:
broken bottles from bootleggers,
rusted guns and ammunition,
maybe torn up wanted posters—

maybe evens lots of bullet holes.

3/19/2021

On a Bike

I might have said it then,
back in the Fifties,
shouted, really, "Hit it, B.J. Ride!"
But everything was so easy then.

Rain had filled the intersection
at the bottom of a hill
a little distance from our junior high,
and the sun swam
in its slow laps from east to west
and back again.

We pedaled fat-tired bikes
straight into a yellow light
that was flashing in our way.

"Forget the depth," we thought.
We knew that we would make it through
The sun's bright image vanished
in a spray of water colored brown.

How many times did we
speed down the hill?
I don't recall,
but there was cleanup,
always cleanup after wild careens.

I'd like to shout
those same words to you

once again, so we could fill
the morning air with laughter
on one more hilarious descent.
But you didn't make it through
one intersection in your life
years ago, in Colorado.

We may not move
at daring speeds.
Gears clog, you know,
not so much with mud—
but with caring—
caring for a time
when any one of us could
wake up the neighbors shouting,
"Hit it, B.J.
Ride!"

8/20/2020

Alpine Park

At least he can return in memory
to where he was a kid,
return to August heat
on long walks made
almost without thought
to a limestone shelter by the creek.
He remembers welcome shade,
stone benches by the wall,
a cool pump handle's touch.

He recalls the kind of ritual
he began in Alpine:
coming in his late teens
with a girl to walk the parkland,
years later, taking the same pathways
with a wife, and later still,
showing the creek and forest
he loved to his child.

She recognized the ceremony,
simple as it was,
they enacted in that shelter
as they took turns
at the pump handle
pouring water on each other's hands.

1/6/2019

What the Dog Said

Yes. Yes.
I recognize you,
though I'm jumping up and down
and barking myself hoarse
at the end of this damned chain.

You're a sweaty, sour-smelling mess
returning from your last
march with a high school band
and wondering what to do
once you give up the uniform.

I'll bet you'll plunk your butt
down on the porch for days
to water crab grass
and snack on fears
of flunking out of university.

It's summer, kid.
Come on!
I'm a constant in your life,
somebody you have loved,
a blessing, yes—
if only for a while.

Take this blessing
for a walk.

It's not just me
who needs to romp.

4/19/2020

At Nineteen

At nineteen, you know
that almost anything can happen here:
You've read half a dozen books on UFOs.
You're sure the proof is in!

You know your country's bound at last
to make a rocket jump straight up
without someone pushing "Self-Destruct"
and head for outer space.
A few years more, and you will see—
the White House promised this—
men bounce across the surface of the Moon.

But just now,
you look out across the Mississippi
and Missouri's darkened plain
where strange lights,
red, green, and white, appear
in patterns you don't recognize.
They wink on and off against the Milky Way.

Could this be it,
a visitation from the neighbors
in a different galaxy?
And could this girl on your arm—
more exciting than anyone
who has traveled lightyears—

be the one thing you did not expect,
someone landing softly
on the rough gravel of your life?

After Retirement

That autumn morning
he stared hard to see
how sunlight made its advance
across the parking lot
in front of his café.
Steam from his usual coffee,
a latte with a double shot,
curled slowly toward the ceiling.
An old westbound bus
turned sharply at the corner
before it made a temporary stop.
Men to his left and right,
leaving half-finished cups on tables
rushed the door.

3/25/2021

Man on Cliff at Iceland's Golden Falls

Welcome Back

You're welcomed back right from the start:
Someone's waiting at the gate to meet you.
"Drive in," they say,
"Pull your car up at a dorm,"
but your wife will do this.
She and the state declared
you cannot take the wheel.

It's not the place
you knew at twenty-one,
but there's consolation
in promised tours and concerts,
old friends, retired profs you love,
desserts to send you straight to dieting,
new people in administration
who come with a surprise:
They all have hair.

They want to make you feel
you can sing the school anthem
in the same key as fifty years ago,
can find again the dirt road to the village,
locate at least one book where they
got rid of Dewey's numbering.

Conversations take you back and back
to when women whose faces
you recall filled the air

with the music of their laughter.
You want to hear what's been
obscured by their new tremolos.
What's left that has not changed?
The river once again in flood,
and stranded groups of trees
across Missouri's plain
that make you think of archipelagos.

There is the line of ragged bluffs as well.
You climbed it more than once
against all college rules.
Like so many places in your life
well after graduation, there were
too few handholds,
at least too few you recognized,
that offered safety.

How is it that you didn't fall?
How is it that you're here?

8/19/2019

Buck House, Principia College, Elsah, Illinois

V

Grandfather Eric

You could have done
anything you wanted to:
painted the kitchen yellow,
the color your wife hated,
ignored her decades-long
commitment to sky blue.

You could have stayed out each night
until someone, Bengston, maybe,
the barman bachelor
who lived above an old maid's place,
turned lights out at the club.

You could have emptied out
the fridge of beer
and returned to aqua vitae and schnapps,
the stuff you used to knock back
with the boys you never spoke about,
when you and they
got dressed up on Saturdays in Sweden,
and, for a while, almost forgot
just where and who you were.

You could have started playing
once again for cash at Euchre
instead of candy.
You could have stopped working

at Republic Furniture.
You could have sold up.

And on one day in 1960,
you could have said almost anything.

The young clerk
at the hospital we all called Swede's
was not wise enough
to stop repeating policy.
You could have shouted,
"You can damn well
wait for money!"
But you did not.

You said instead,
"Send me the bill.
I did not expect
to walk out of here alone."

You did not know
that for a couple years
you would choose to walk
into the whine of shop saws
to bring your lathe to life.
Your heart would not let you
give up making things
that were beautiful.

You didn't know
you would paint the upstairs green
with the trim in pink,
that you would leave the kitchen blue
or that you would
keep Ina's flower garden bright.

But most of all,
you didn't know you would bring
the gift of quiet,
as if you had shaped it especially
for each one of us,
and placed it gently
in our hands.

4/20/2020

For Great Uncle Hjalmar

I have your watch, I think,
unless great grandchildren
carried it away,
your chest of drawers—
or was it Eric's?
Tobacco left its scent
on felt for over 90 years,
and here's your snuff box
and one gold-plated knife.

I have no photograph,
no memories of you.
So few words about you
have been handed down:

You had a millwright job.
You built a boat for tourists
to travel up and down the Rock.

Your crazy sister Anna
lost the history of the family
you spent years in writing down.

You never wed,
unless it was the aqua vitae,
and now the lines of text about you
on your headstone

are smoothing out
like your boat wake on the river
as it slowly moved downstream.

4/18/2020

Grandfather Anton

You kept your heart
where you felt almost whole,
employed, in reading.
Your cut-off schooling
in the 1890's made you mad to find
some explanation of your life.

So, you kept reading
late into night past milking time,
late into day,
past time for slopping hogs
about a world that would arrive
(Had not the prophet Marx foretold it?)
and a world that was bound to go away.

You read the books you found in trash,
whatever house sales let go cheap:
assorted out-of-date biographies
accounts of savage revolutions,
the histories of European wars,
and lost kingdoms in the sea.

You lost the first farm by the river,
the second farm as well,
then moved to town
with three children and a cursing wife.

You kept reading
after you invented drills

to make the work go quickly on the shop floor
for your comrades and yourself.

You found both solace and intoxicant
in knowing how the world must be.

You should have kept to reading, Anton,
let history play out.

They slammed the shop doors hard
behind you in the city
when a foreman heard you quoting Marx.

They gave you time,
oh, so much unpaid, unwanted time,
not meant to read,
but to figure out your life.

4/18/2020

Grandmother Hilma

Morning once again,
and I have failed again to throw
the dishes out.

Anton touches Molly's head
as if, before a day in harness
in this heat,
he might comfort her.

Why does it take so long
for that man traveling with his camera
to take another photograph
we cannot afford?

The reins lie slack in my hands,
but in the picture
it will look as if
I'm all dressed up
to drive the wagon into Belvedere.

No whip today to lash the horses:
It seems a wagonload of fire
moves high above this prairie
toward the West.
I cannot chase it in its run.

3/19/2021

Great Aunt Anna

Carl's gone,
gone now for years,
and that widow woman
down on Fifth,
the one he never said he loved but did.
And he thought
I was too dumb to know a thing.

Do I have kids?
He wanted none of that.
Perhaps by accident
he had a few with someone else.

See here.
I have a fridge.
Take what you like;
there's herring, farm cheese,
hard tack.
I'll boil up some Folgers
for you in the pot.

But before this day
gets me down with too much heat
I must go out.
The landlord's saving money,
won't hire the boy next door
to cut my little plot of grass.

Hand me the pinking shears.
Don't worry.
I still can get down on my knees.

VI

Some Cartage Company Family Members

The Trial

They had him dead to rights.
He could not meet their eyes
where they were holding court.

Eight hundred dollars missing
from the cartage company they'd built
hoping to make a decent living
out of hauling freight.

Their semi-truck would soon be gone
through repossession.
Yet no one spoke
of phoning for the cops.
They too had wives and kids,
but not his bills,
no, nothing like his bills.

My father never told me
who stole the money they all needed
or why he would not speak his name.

They all felt dark winds in the Thirties
blowing like a judgment
tearing hearts and lives
and livelihoods away.
Why should they not allow a man
to clutch his name?

3/19/2021

Figure in the Snow

In pre-dawn dark,
you're glad to see the snow
as it falls almost shyly
to the ground.
The night's great storm has passed
and left you work to do.

The shovel in your hand
will lift and pitch this burden,
lift and pitch again.
Great drifts demand you work
by feel to find the way
you need to go.

Just now, you think
it's how you live your life.

You tell yourself
too many times each day,
"You did your time,"
and most people in the congregation
have seen it outlined
in the hollows of your face.
They say they're glad
to give you work.
You know there's time when you have
finished with the walks and drive

to look into the swirling sky
and let the thinning snow descend
on you and everything with grace,
time as well to drop backwards
on the snow, stretch out
against the church lawn's white,
time before the neighbors wake
and walk the path you cleared.

Perhaps they'll wonder why some man
outlined himself in snow
but didn't try to
make the angel wings.

You'll never ask that of yourself:
So many years inside—
so many years.

A man must fill
the empty places in his life.

9/17/2020

Unprepared

We weren't prepared for winter in the city,
for cars and trucks affording no escape,
locked up in snowy mounds on Parkavash.
We weren't prepared for TV's sunny tales
of life with Gilligan
or "Love Boat's" brief amours.

We weren't prepared
for how old angers blew
like powdered snow
around the house.

We weren't prepared with anything
that could move us
toward each other in the cold.

We prayed to hear the sound
of metal scraping pavement,
for the glare of work lights
flashing in the dark.

At dawn, we woke to find
a sky that took its time
in thinning out its metal gray
to show some hints of blue.

We spotted neighbors
trudging down our street

not yet ploughed clear.
They must have been
more ready, more prepared
than we were
for the heart of winter.

They headed straight for Kroger's,
moving past our windows slowly,
mittened hand in hand.

7/14/2020

The Lockers

He used to know his locker number
in its secluded place along the wall.
And for three years
he knew a few things
he needed to keep safe.

He used to know the easy ways to class:
Band, Math, Physics, German, History.
He used to know each place
that he was meant to go,
the way light fell on winter days,
how all things had their place and pace
set by a buzzer or a bell.

He used to know the distance
to the door.
He'd paced it off,
expecting that there'd be
a May-bright afternoon
when he'd walk out
and hear the crash door slam.

But how could he foresee
the final afternoon that opened
to a maze of streets and walks
and trash-filled alleyways
that might lead anywhere?
One led him—and a daughter—

to a place a hundred stories up
beneath a burnt orange sky
to see Chicago sprawling
in its grid North and South and West,
and eastward toward the
darkness of the lake.

How had he reached this place
to stare with her at what seemed
a patterned world?
How hope that she would find a locker
for her heart before she'd
walk out into her own bright May?

7/18/2020

Descending with the Goth

With speed
you descend,
getting on at 23,
don't smile, don't talk,
and don't appear to listen,
stare straight ahead at steel.

I study how your dark hair
sweeps black and shining
part way down
the long curve of your back.

I failed to notice
when you entered
if you wore eyeliner,
emphatic in its red and black,
the gaudy needlework of tattooing,
or if you had decided
some part of you
should be pierced with nails.

Old men do these things,
you know,
sometimes—
look long
and perhaps desperately
at women,
remembering how someone

half your age
stood in too many elevators
looking up
below her baseball cap
at numbers racing
in an ascent
to gleaming corridors.

You walk out
to summer grass,
and soft
touch of rain,
your black shirt announcing
"Love kills slowly,"
as if it were the final diagnosis.

Daughter,
get the damned text right,
and do it quickly.

It isn't love that slowly kills.

It's grief.

5/20/2020

VII

Boss Lady

Just yesterday,
the world we were sure of
started losing definition.
All day we watched hard rain
blur the edges of ice-crusted drifts
before they began, like us, to slump.

It's not that Spring in muddy boots
strode in to startle us,
but you,
you early, and
on three-inch heels.

You ordered up
so many things for us to do
because you knew some jargon
belonging to our craft.
So, on the drive home in the evening,
Peg and I laughed
at almost everything but grief.

Did you order us to make a filing system
from a simple word processor?
teach four different PC systems
to six blind people all at once?
I'm not sure,
but it all seems likely now.

Or was it only that you wanted
us find the right job
for a blind guy at the Center
who said he read what God wrote him
in Braille's own kind of shorthand
in rough plaster on the wall?

3/19/2021

The Placement Department Secretary

Well, Rick is 46, you know,
Tech Department head, divorced,
and so, what do you think I'd ask
when he'd gone off
with his new helper—
with her short skirts—
to that tech conference for a week?
"Did you get anywhere with Lynn?"

Maybe he's a faker—
or some Goody-Two Shoes.
He looked like I just hit him with a brick.

I asked her that same thing
when she came in today,
"Did Rick get anywhere with you?"
And for a whole minute
it seemed she didn't understand.

What did she learn in college anyway?

I've got to get a new job.
I don't understand these people.

Have you got a light?"

3/19/2021

In the Piano Tuning School

The woman in the fur coat
could have turned away,
said nothing or spoken later
on the quiet to the man
who drove her to this
training center for the blind,
but she was on a tour
for the philanthropic-minded
who must see all things for themselves
and say later to their friends
what the world is really like.

"They have their little jobs," she said,
uncertain what they really were,
and the students heard her say it softly
as she closed their lunchroom door.

They snapped lunch boxes shut,
grabbed long white canes
and returned to picking through the tools
of what would be their future trade.

Some cursed and yanked
piano octaves high
on aged instruments,
too high to get a decent temperament,
but too low to break a string.
In silence, others sorted out

the piles of wooden flanges
they'd learned to make
revolve with ease
around bright little pins.

It would be like this a long time,
as if they did not know it—
burnishing the needed
small things of the world.

3/19/2021

Sensitivity Training Day

You are supposed to represent the blind
at Bell Labs in Illinois,
so, don't make a mess of it.
And everyone's involved.
Develop sensitivity.
Yes. Theirs.

A woman who is a deaf-mute
from the Living Center
gets to the heart of things,
and signs to her interpreter,
"In any place that's new
I have to write things out.
"'Just point me to the john.'"

The woman in a powered chair
makes things more explicit.
"I can find it well enough,
but damned if I can get in."

It's your turn now to offer
any insight that you can.

"Marty writes out her need for help
and hopes at least for pointing
or something put in print.
And Rachel can't get through
doors that must seem built

to keep her out."
 "I can ask anybody
I hear speaking,
where to go, but all they say is,
""It is over there.""

"Oh, all we want
is what you want as well:
to reach a place
that offers quiet
to do what's needed,
and—face it!—
escape for whole minutes
just to think,
wash up,
or maybe check
a message from someone
who knows how to reach us,

take a breath,

get back to work.

5/26/2020

Entering the Training Center for the Blind

You don't have to look too far
for what might scare you here.
An old man in dark glasses
double-hands the wall
as he tries to find an office door,
but no one tells him what to do
or tries to stop
the progress of his fear.

This is your first but not
your last visit as a squinter
to a training center for the blind,
and you don't know
what anyone in charge
is going to see in you.

Someone will call your name,
and may fail to say it right,
but don't tell them how to say it now.
Head straight to Intake and show off.
Spot the big "E" on the Snellen chart,
maybe F P, even T O Z below.

They say they'll test you later
on some things you know
you sure as hell don't want:
a blindfold and a white cane.
You don't want to learn

the stillness you would need
to let you find yourself in space

by hearing faint sounds
returning from a wall.

You don't want to learn
the use of making wide arcs
with a white cane
on a crowded street to
make people give you way.

You feel too well the fears
of clinic staff.
There's nothing said aloud,
but what they fear is always about light,
that it may, for you, for them,
and lastly, for the cosmos,
all go out.
There's no movement in a vision
dark as that.

Tap the long cane that they gave you
against the wall that's nearest.
Trace it to the far end.
Find a door that opens.
Right now.
Move!

3/19/2021

Sunday 2 a.m.

My God! man.
You just woke me up
whispering, "Dummy, Dummy!
to the darkness and yourself.

You've got a small
new Braille computer
resting on the quilt
above you on your bed.
I hear faint taps of keys,
the spacebar's click,
the sound your fingers make
as they brush raised dots forming
and un-forming tactile messages
you don't want to read.

Don't you know it's late,
that we're both off the clock
for checking if new hardware works.

No one will pay attention
if we don't find the glitches
in computers or ourselves.

We can test the new stuff
if we're asked to in the morning,
make corrections to the manuals
that may open up to, say, page 32

and tell us late, too late about
"the first thing you should do…"
Well, we can give advice—yes!—
give it kindly
when we need to.

There's time, real time,
for handling all of that.
It's the logic of our business.

And time too
for another kind of work
we all may do at times.

It's difficult as always.
and won't be recognized
if we stare up at night,
touch gingerly the past in memory
and its unwelcome messages,
choose to say or not to say,
"Dummy! Dummy!" to the darkness
and ourselves.

3/30/2020

By the Fox River

His wife swings her white cane
left and right to find
the edges of their path
and says, "I hear some geese.
They're straight ahead."

He swings up the lenses
of his old binoculars
to find the geese but sees
instead, a woman
with tan, enormous breasts—
and she's staring back.

Perhaps she sees his thick glasses
and the woman
with a long cane at his side,
then makes sense of everything,
but he thinks that she will yell,
"Just who in hell are you?"
And he's aware
he cannot answer that.

He turns the lenses swiftly right,
just guessing where the birds must be,
and tells his wife,
"The geese are on the riverbank,
just waddling around."

So easy, he thinks then, to check
the edges of a path,
not what's straight ahead.

1/12/17/2021

The Old Finnish Trapper

"Once caught in a trap," he said,
"a coyote will give up—
just give up and look back at you
right down your rifle sights
and wait for you to pull the trigger."

I've not encountered such passivity,
but that is what the trapper said.

That is what he said while,
patient, year on year,
he pried apart—
or tried to open up
steel jaws of disabilities and griefs
that held fast the people
that he loved.

He kept praying
for an intervening grace
even as he said this,
"Time always keeps me firmly
in its sights."

31/19/2020

VIII

Marching military cadets in Hanoi

Night Blindness

Sir, this is not Vietnam.
We are not blinded by the night.

Once the sun drops out of sight,
the world, for us, turns green, not
black and white or gray.
And, soon after, green figures
with green rifles, RPGs or mortars skulk
among green houses, across rooftops,
between the many greening graves.

Of course, we report all we see
as hostiles to H.Q.
An order comes.
We light 'em up.

Then nothing moves,
at least not for a while, but us.
No. I can't tell you
how long it takes us to adjust to
night-fighting there.

There is such searing fire
from gunships we keep our goggles on
to avoid the dark of after-images.

They arrive at dawn.

1/12/2021

A Late Note to Ismat

Ismat, they loved you, man,
though they, like me,
could not pronounce your name
unless you said it several times.

They loved you, man.
They never thought they'd see
a young Pakistani guy
jump straight up on a bar
below a muted TV set
and start talking down Khomeini—
and the men who torched
our consulate
in your own country too.
You countered what they argued
from the Koran
verse by verse by verse.

Ismat, they loved you, man.
You lit up the way it was out there,
the places that none of us
could locate on a map
or imagine we would ever go.

Ismat, they loved you, man,
a guy who knew to cheer
the Cubs, the Bears,

a guy who held his Bud—
or was it Heineken?

They loved you, man,
and raised you on their shoulders,
drove you from bar to bar downtown.
Were you surprised
when women rushed to kiss you?

Are you in Karachi now
or perhaps Islamabad?

It's decades late to ask:

When you were walking in the market
or down a narrow lane
what was it like when someone
close behind you
spoke your name?

9/27/2020

Some Questions from the Readjustment Counselor

Was there light enough to see
when you entered that strange country,
the one you never heard about at school?

What sounds let you know
you were not at home?

Do some sights or smells
still linger in your memory?
Are there any that you wish
would go away?

Before you left,
did anyone describe the place
to which you said
you felt consigned?

Was its safety doubtful
even in your early days?

It was hard duty, wasn't it,
finding day by day,
you'd be taking fire
at almost every intersection of your life,
taking fire from those you thought
you were meant to save?

Was there mining going on below you,
or other kinds of sabotage?

Did you have to learn
some counter-mining skills?

Describe the day you knew
you'd had too many losses,
had heard too many times,
"what we do
don't mean nothin' here,"
the time before you broke out
of what you've called
your regimented life,
the time before
you met the village girl.

What was it like the day
her child arrived?
Did he have your eyes?

She must have had your heart.
I see in paperwork
you've asked if she
can join you.

You are in your own country now,
and close to home.

Can you give her light enough
to see how things will be here—
if she comes?

1/12/2021

Delivering Bad News

Whatever hurts the heart may come in bursts,
but those who bring the news may be afraid
of how you may reply, let's say, to these:
"Your house just burned!" or something worse:
"Your son's been killed in a jihadist raid.
Gunships came in too late above the trees."

And after such announcements you restart
your life again—or die—or maybe fade away,
declining to take part in history.
But know whoever brings bad news can smart,
distressed there's little comforting to say.
You both may hate the loss and mystery.

Speaker or hearer, take your part
Remember bad news travels heart to heart.

1/13/2021

An Apostrophe to Pastor Bob

On Sunday mornings you stood up to shout
about the End of Times, about the Crown
of who'd be going up or going down.
That's what the "Final Judgment" was about.

Most days, the congregation hoped they'd sing
so loud they'd drown their grand piano out,
but there were days the drive filled up with louts
who honked their horns in chorus just to bring

some damn fool out who'd chase them down the road.
Once he caught up, they'd hit him with a bat.
You chased them, hoped to talk; they knocked you flat.
That made you question lots of Christian codes.

Healed up, you grabbed a shotgun. Then you said,
"Why fool with those young hoodlums anymore?
I'll shoot their tires with my double-bore,"
and preached with gusto of the quick and dead.

Cops found the men who hit you, scarred your face.
You never quite explained what happened then.
In place of vicious punks, did you see men
whom jails might harden, even keep from Grace?

Who understood your Final Judgment business?
For gross assault, you offered them forgiveness'.

10/12/2020

Rain in the Valley

In whatever years may come
when the land is out of breath
because the sky is unforgiving,

when spillways fall away
to shattered rocks that shine
and pulse with heat,

when words transform themselves
to sharpened implements
with which we cut ourselves
or hurl at those who love us,

let me remember
how the Shenandoah rushed the valley
from its springs in Rockingham,

when thinning veils
of water vanished in flood at the lip
of this, the Burnshire Dam,

when we knew
we could open up our mouths
wide enough to bless,
wide enough to sing.

Can we trust the covenant
between sun and water
won't be seem forever broken?

Can we trust at least the heart?
Like earth, it has its
own burning times,
may lie blackened, desolate,
have its sweet springs filled in
by fear or hate.

Who will say, once found,
the heart's springs
can't be opened
or that someday
we will not hear
within ourselves a voice,
ignored perhaps for centuries,
declare, "The heart has streams
that offer life.
Dig there."

5/26/2020

The photographs included in this book were taken by the author
or family members at various times and places.

This book is about personal movements—
in space, between countries—
in time, between memories of real and imagined individuals—
between vastly different careers—
between visions of how we live in and care for
each other and the world.

Printed in the United States
by Baker & Taylor Publisher Services